365 Sayings of Prophet Muhammad

(*Peace be upon him*)

Compiled and Translated by

Abdur Raheem Kidwai

JAICO PUBLISHING HOUSE

Ahmedabad Bangalore Bhopal Bhubaneswar Chennai
Delhi Hyderabad Kolkata Lucknow Mumbai

Published by Jaico Publishing House
A-2 Jash Chambers, 7-A Sir Phirozshah Mehta Road
Fort, Mumbai - 400 001
jaicopub@jaicobooks.com
www.jaicobooks.com

365 SAYINGS OF PROPHET MUHAMMAD
ISBN 978-81-7992-838-7

First Jaico Impression: 2008
Seventh Jaico Impression: 2014

There is an excellent example (of conduct) for you in Prophet Muhammad, God's Messenger.

The Quran 33:21

CONTENTS

KEY TO ABBREVIATIONS

The following abbreviations have been used in the present work for indicating the source/s of the Prophet's Sayings. Reference is to the compilors or titles of major collections of *Hadith* (the Prophet's Sayings):

A = Ahmad

B = Bukhari

BQ = Bayhaqi

D = Abu Dawud

I = Ibn Majah

M = Muslim

MK = Malik

MSH = *Mishkat al-Masabih*

N = Nasai

T = Tirmidhi

PREFACE

The present work seeks to familiarize readers with one of the primary sources of Islamic faith and practice ________ *Hadith* (Prophet Muhammad's Sayings). His Sayings, reflecting profound wisdom and pure morality, have been one of the main sources of guidance and law for Muslims of all time and place from the early days of Islam up to the present time. His Sayings represent the elaboration of the truths contained in the Quran, the Word of God revealed to Prophet Muhammd (peace be upon him). It is not therefore surprising that a point hinted at in the Quran gets amplified in the Prophet's Sayings. Likewise, one notes some of the Quranic precepts articulated in a different way in his Sayings. Early Muslims recognized well the Prophet's role in the divine scheme of things. For, he helped them see and follow the way prescribed by God for earning His pleasure, which, in turn, brought to them abiding success in both the worlds.

Since the Prophet (peace be upon him) was their role model, and continues to be so up to this day for more than one billion Muslims the world over, they tried their level best to emulate him. Their relationship with him is captured in the following account:

All his actions served them as a precedent (*sunnah*), every word falling from his lips to them, and all his actions were virtuous in their eyes, which they wanted to follow as faithfully as they could. When he chose a gold ring for himself, his friends also put it on; and when he put it off, they threw it away, and put on a silver ring instead, they also followed his example. If he offered prayers at midnight, all his friends wanted to do the same, and himself had to stop them from so doing. If he fasted continuously for more than a day, his followers also desired to do the same, and he had to explain to them his special privileges. Zayd b. Khalid spent one whole night at his door in order to see him offer his night prayers. Nawwas b. Sam'an stayed at Madinah for one whole year in order to enquire from him what was virtue and what was vice. Abu Sa'id al-Khudri observed keenly how long he kept standing in his afternoon prayers. Ibn 'Umar counted how many times he asked pardon of God in one sitting.

Moreover, apart from conveying the divine message, as a social reformer and spiritual mentor *par excellence* he brought about their moral transformation and spiritual regeneration. Throughout his Prophetic career, he instructed them day and night in every walk of life, illustrating what should be done and what be avoided. It went a long way in instilling the conviction among his followers that all of their actions, no matter how trivial these might appear to them, are closely watched by God, and that they do or fail to do. These early Muslims and their subsequent generations took every possible step to record all the directives of the Prophet (peace be upon him), which constitute Hadith corpus.

Another purpose likely to be served by this selection is to help readers gain or renew their acquaintance with Prophet Muhammad (peace be upon him), one of the most influential figures in history, who has influenced human thought and life, and whose career stands out for his astounding success. His Sayings on a wide range of topics and issues, as recorded in this work, provide a glimpse of his mind – his overflowing love and affection for mankind, especially for the weak, the poor, orphans and women; his committment to fairness and social justice for all; his modesty and simplicity, reflected particularly in his repeated directives that he be not idolized or extolled, as he took great pride in being only a servant of God and, above all, his ardent desire for promoting true faith, high morals and manners and excellent conduct.

This selection of the Prophet's Sayings aims also at outlining the Islamic worldview, presenting a conspectus of Islamic code of conduct governing every Muslim's family, social, political, economic and spiritual life. Non-Muslims may find it as a useful introduction to both Islamic faith and practices. Throughout this work the focus is on illustrating the Prophet's guidelines for leading life at both individual and collective levels. Some of his directives are inevitably specific to Muslim community, as for example, those which deal with the articles of Islamic faith and the Hereafter. Strikingly enough, most of his directives are marked by a broad, general thrust in asking Muslims to lead their lives in a pluralistic polity signifying the wider community of all the men and women, irrespective of their faith in that all of them happen to be the servants and creatures of the One True God. Equally valid and relevant are his directives for non-Muslim as well. It would not be surprising if non-Muslim readers are struck by the Prophet's catholicity of mind and his sincere, genuine concern for the welfare and happiness of humanity at large. Some of his observations stand out for his accurate predictions. Take the following as instances in point which have almost come true in our time.

- There would be a time when the killer would not know as to why he killed someone and his victims would have no idea as to why they were killed.
- There would come a time when people would turn wholly indifferent to the issue whether their income is lawful or not.

While every care has been taken to present a largely faithful translation of the Prophet's Sayings, originally in Arabic, some of these appear in somewhat abridged forms. At times, the import of his Sayings has been paraphrased, without deviating considerably from the original.

It is hoped the readers, Muslims and non-Muslim alike, would profit much from the Prophet's life-enriching guidance. A little effort on our part in acting on his directives is bound to bring about a sea-change in our outlook on life, improve vastly our conduct and imbue our personal lives, our society and our broader community life with peace and joy.

I must thank Mr. R.H. Sharma, Jaico Publishing House, Mumbai for asking me to compile this work, as part of the excellent *365 Sayings Series*. Mr. Sharma's initiative deserves great appreciation. It would go a long way in forging cordial Inter Faith relations and better understanding of major world faiths.

While pronouncing or writing the name of any Messenger of God, Muslims use the honorific formula "peace be upon him". The same norm is followed in this book. Any suggestion for improving this book is highly welcome.

Abdur Raheem Kidwai
Aligarh Muslim University, Aligarh
sulaim_05@yahoo.co.in

INTRODUCTION

In the Islamic scheme of things Prophet Muhammad (peace be upon him) occupies a pivotal position. It is one of the essential articles of faith for Muslims to believe in and abide by all that the Prophet (peace be upon him) said or did. His actions and sayings, referred to in Islamic terminology as *Sunnah* and *Hadith* respectively, are, therefore, of great importance and relevance for Muslims of all time and place. Muslims' esteem for the Prophet (peace be upon him) does not hinge on personality cult or idolizing him. Rather, they cannot profess and practise Islam without drawing upon the example set by the Prophet (peace be upon him). The following account brings into sharper focus the significance of the Prophet's Sayings in the broader world context of Islam.

According to the Quran, the Islamic Scripture, God sent down Prophet Muhammad (peace be upon him) in order to "teach them the Book and wisdom" (al-Jumu'ah 62:2). At another place, the Quran outlines his role: "God has sent down this Reminder (the Quran) upon you that you may elucidate to the people the teaching that has been sent down for them." (al-Nahl 16: 44). The same truth is pressed home thus: "We sent among you a Messenger of yourselves, who recites to you our signs, purifies you, instructs you in the Book and in wisdom, and teaches you what you did not know." (al-Baqarah 2: 151). It is not therefore surprising that on being asked to spell out the Prophet's conduct, Aishah, his wife readily answered that he demonstrated in his everyday life what the Quran preaches theoretically. The Islamic modes of worship, moral code, socio-political ideals, thought patterns, concern for the Hereafter and spiritual outlook were put into practice by him, which served as a living role model for all the early Muslims who came to know or hear about him.

The Quran contains several directives urging Muslims to be kind to the orphan, the poor, the elderly, women and children. However, they imbibed this moral lesson in the real sense on observing first-hand the Prophet's overflowing love and affection for these sections of the society. They saw with their own eyes that he used to skip meals in order to feed the needy. He led a frugal life while he generously helped the poor and the weak. Never did he hit or take revenge against anyone, though he had been persecuted for years. They noted amazingly how he spent his time on visiting the sick, joining funeral and consoling those in distress. As the head of his household, and as father, husband and neighbour he set for them an example how to perform these basic familial and social roles. His directives in the above real life situations were closely observed and faithfully followed by his companions. More significantly, they asked their subsequent generations to emulate the same. This explains why the Prophet's Sayings carry the pride of place in the Islamic scheme of things.

Another instance in point is afforded by the Quranic command for liturgical Prayer, which underscores his central role in things Islamic. The Quran obliges every Muslim to offer Prayers everyday. However, he it was who illustrated all the aspects of this command: time, place, number, rituals, and method of offering Prayers. Through his example Muslims realized the effectiveness of Prayer in moulding their outlook on life. His Sayings thus set the agenda for professing and practising Islam.

Of all the Messengers of God, Prophet Muhammad (peace be upon him) holds the distinction of being the last and final bearer of God's guidance for mankind. More significantly, he is the only Messenger whose entire Prophetic career is meticulously preserved in writing. All that he said, did, approved or disapproved even by his slight gesture and body language is on record. From the beginning of his mission, a host of his followers devoted themselves fully to recording and transmitting faithfully to posterity his Sayings. With the passage of time this exercise gained in depth and rootage. Hadith sciences soon developed into one of the most extensive branches of learning in Islamic tradition. Some of the best Muslim minds collected, edited and promoted Hadith studies. This trend continues up to this day, and has contributed much to the popularity and importance of the Prophet's Sayings among Muslims across the world.

Muslims believe that the Prophet (peace be upon him) being constantly under God's care and supervision while discharging his Prophetic duty, was inspired and guided by God in all of his actions. Accordingly Muslims are obliged to abide by his directives, besides those ordained by the Quran. The divine revelation constitutes what we know as the Quran whereas the special knowledge imparted to the Prophet (peace be upon him) by God, which is reflected in his actions and sayings, represents what the Quran brands as "wisdom". Imparting wisdom is specifically and recurrently mentioned in the Quran as the Prophet's main assignment: "God has revealed to you the Book and wisdom, and He taught you what you did not know." (al-Nisa 4:113). Elsewhere, the Prophet's family members are as reminded of the divine favours bestowed upon them: "Remember the signs of God and the words of wisdom which are rehearsed in your homes." (al-Ahazab 33:34). "Wisdom" in the above instance signifies the Prophet's words and deeds. It explains also why it is so important to learn about and act upon the Prophet's Sayings.

God in the Quran both sanctions and sanctifies the Prophet's way in this proclamation:

As for him who sets himself against the Prophet and follows a path other than that of the believers even after true guidance has become clear to him, God will let him go the way he has turned to, and will cast him into Hell—an evil destination.

The Quran 4:115

Numerous instances in early Islamic history corroborate the point that Muslim rulers were guided by the Prophet's rulings and sayings in deciding any matter. It is on record about Caliph Abu Bakr that he publicly asked about the Prophet's precedent on any issue which was not in his knowledge. On coming to know it, he decided the matter accordingly. Same holds true of both the Muslim rulers and masses of a later date. They are guided by the Prophet's directives in all aspects of their life. This brings out the significance and relevance of his Sayings in both the Islamic scheme of things and in the lives of more than one billion Muslims in the world today.

Amid many collections of the Prophet's Sayings, edited assiduously by several scholars in the early history of Islam, the following deserve mention. Those interested in the subject would find their study rewarding:

Bukhari's *al-Jami' al-Sahih*

Abu Abdullah ibn Ismail al-Bukhari (810-870), of Persian descent was born in Bukhara, now in Central Asia. God had blessed him with strong intellect and sharp retentive memory which contributed much to his fame later as one of the towering Hadith scholars. In his forty years long search for collecting the Prophet's Sayings, he visited almost all the important centres of Islamic learning located in different parts of the Muslim world. For example, he stayed at Basra for five years, in Hijaz, part of the present day Saudi Arabia for six years and traveled several times to Egypt, Kufa and Baghdad. The fruits of his diligent scholarship are embodied in his collection *Sahih al-Bukhari,* containing his careful selection of 7275 thematically arranged Sayings of the Prophet (peace be upon him). These are subdivided into 100 sections and 3450 chapters.

Muslim's *Sahih*

Sahih Muslim, another major Hadith collection by Abu Husain Asakir Muslim b. Hajjaj (817-874), is next only to Bukhari's *Sahih.* Muslim was born in Nishapur and traveled widely in Persia, Iraq, Syria and Egypt for mastering the discipline of Hadith. After examining a large number of the Sayings, he finally selected 4000 authentic reports which feature in his collection.

Abu Dawud's *Sunan*

Abu Dawud Sulayman ibn al-Ashtah (817-888) of Arab stock, was born most probably in Basra. He pursued the study of Hadith in Arabia, Persia, Syria and Egypt and tried to gather all the reported Sayings of the Prophet (peace be upon him). His collection, *Sunan* retains the meticulous standards of scholarship found in the works of Bukhari and Muslim. However, his collection includes some of the reports which are not regarded as reliable by some scholars. Abu Dawud, nonetheless, does well in pointing out the defects in such reports.

Tirmidhi's *Jami*

As an illustrious student of Abu Dawud, Abu Isa Muhammad ibn Isa (821-892) carried further the work of his teacher and spiritual master. He learnt Hadith at the feet of Bukhari and Muslim. His labeling of reports as genuine or otherwise is one of the most valuable elements of his work.

Nasai's *Sunan*

Abu Abd al-Rahman Ahmad ibn Shuayb al-Nasai (827-915) hailed from Khurasan. He studied Hadith in Central Asia and visited Egypt and Syria for collecting Hadith. His *Sunan,* a large collection of the Prophet's Sayings, is one of the six standard works on the subject. A striking feature of this work is that it contains variants of many Hadith reports, followed by Nasai's comments on the authenticity or otherwise of each report.

Ibn Maja's *Sunan*

Abu Abdullah Muhammad ibn Yazid, popularly known as Ibn Maja (822- 887) was born at Qazwin, Persia. For gaining thorough knowledge of Hadith he visited Persia, Iraq, Syria, Arabia and Egypt. Contained in his collection are 4000 Sayings of the Prophet (peace be upon him) placed into 32 sections and 1500 chapters.

Bayhaqi's *Sunan*

Abu Bakr Ahmad ibn al-Husain of Nishapur, popularly known as Bayhaqi learnt Hadith at the feet of many eminent scholars. His *Sunan* stands out for its thematic arrangement and its method of treating Hadith reports.

Malik's *Muwatta*

Malik ibn Anas (d.795) stands out as a distinguished jurist and Hadith scholar of *Madina*. His collection of Hadith, *Muwatta* contains also the rulings of Madinan jurists. His work is one of the earliest extant writings on Hadith and jurisprudence.

Those interested in further study of the Prophet's Sayings would find the following works in English highly useful:

The Translation of the Meaning of Summarized Sahih Al-Bukhari Translation by Muhammad Muhsin Khan, 1994.

Sahih Al-Bukhari Being Traditions of the Sayings and Doings of the Prophet Translation by Muhammad Asad, 1978.

Sahih Muslim: Abridged Translation by Aftab Shahryar, 2004.

Mishkat Al-Masabih Traslation by James Robson, 1970.

An-Nawawi's Forty Hadith: An Anthology of the Sayings of the Prophet Muhammad, 1997.

Studies in Early Hadith Literature: by Muhammad Mustafa Azami, 1978.

Hadith Literature: Its Origin, Development, Special Features and Criticism by Muhammad Zubair Siddiqui, 1993.

Glimpses of the Hadith by Muhammad Azizullah, 1973.

Human Rights and Obligations, in the light of the Koran and Hadith by Sayyid Sulaiman Nadvi, 1996.

Hadith, Traditions of Prophet Muhammad by Abdur Rahman I. Doi, 1980.

Selection from Hadith by Abdul Hameed Siddiqui, 1979.

Hadith and Sunnah by Mazhrul Haq Qazi and Anis Ahmad, 1999.

Section I

How to live life

1. Morals and Manners

God has sent me down in order to profess and practise moral values and deeds. v

Sharah al-Sunnah

The best among you are those who have excellent character and conduct.

B/M

Many people would be admitted to Paradise on account of their piety and excellent morals and manners. By the same token, many would be consigned to Hell for having not protected their tongues and their private parts.

(T)

Only conduct would carry weight on a believer's scale on the Day of Judgement.

D/T

Among the believers the perfect one is he who excels others in good character and conduct. The best one among you is he who is kind to the women under his care.

(T)

You are not better than any black or white person. If you are pious, this alone makes you better than others.

(A)

Some persons approached the Prophet (peace be upon him), telling him: "The members of Daws tribe have refused to accept Islam. You should pronounce a curse upon them." He replied: "O God! Bless the members of Daws tribe with guidance and draw them closer to me."

(M)

Saying good words is as good as giving charity.

(B)

The best among people is he who is the most pious, God-fearing and truthful. His conduct is not tainted by any sin, injustice, jealousy or rancour.

I/BQ

10

God overlooks the lapses of a person who does not speak ill of others. Likewise, one who controls his anger would be protected from God's punishment on the Day of Judgement. Whoever pleads himself guilty before God, his plea would be accepted by God.

BQ

Avoid suspicion. For suspicion is often baseless. Do not spy on each other. Do not probe others' affairs. Nor should you indulge in worldliness or jealousy. Do not have a grudge against each other. Nor should you betray anyone. Rather, lead life as servants of God and live as brethren.

MK

I have little to do with this world. My worldly life is no more than the sojourn of a traveler, taking rest under the shade of a tree and then moving on immediately.

A/T/I

Once the Prophet (peace be upon him) asked his Companions: "Who do you think is a poor person?" They replied: "One who does not have money or material resources." He, however, clarified: "The poor among my community is he whose record of deeds on the Day of Judgement would, no doubt, include his Prayers, fasting and payment of Zakah. However, his record would list also his misdeeds such as abusing and slandering others, his usurping others' belongings and his hitting or killing people. As a recompense, his good deeds would be credited to the account of his victims. Consequently he would not get any reward for his good acts. If this does not settle his account, even the sins committed by his victims would be transferred to his account, which would lead to his hurling into Hell. This is the person who is really poor."

(M)

14

Jealousy is permissible in the following two cases only:

(i) He, who is blessed by God with wealth, spends it lavishly on the cause of truth, and

(ii) He who is favoured by God with wisdom, decides cases prudently and instructs people in wisdom.

B/A

The Prophet (peace be upon him) recounted the following incident: "Once as a traveler quenched his thirst at a well, he saw a dog panting out of thirst. He offered water in his leather sock to the dog. God appreciated this good deed of his so much that He granted him deliverance." Those present asked in astonishment whether they would get any reward for kindness to animals. He affirmed it strongly, adding that there is divine reward for showing kindness to every living being.

B/M

You are free to eat, drink and dress as it pleases you, as long as you do not betray pride and refrain from extravagance.

(B)

17

These three traits characterize a believer's conduct:

(i) Even in a fit of anger, he does not resort to falsehood.

(ii) Even when he is elated, he does not transgress the bounds of truth.

(iii) When he enjoys power, he does not deny people their due.

MSH

One's wealth does not decrease, as he gives it in God's way. When one gives money in charity, it reaches God even before it is taken by its recipient.

Tabarani

One is rewarded for helping a needy person, who is not his kith and kin. However, he gets a double reward for helping his needy relative; one reward for charity and another for fulfilling obligations towards the ties of kinship.

N/T

On being asked to identify the best charity, the Prophet (peace be upon him) replied: "The charity given to one's poor relative who is hostile to him stands out as the best kind of charity."

Targhib

21

None of you would die before getting all the sustenance which God has already decreed for you. Fear God and employ only fair means for getting your bread. Any delay in securing your sustenance should not prompt you to use unfair means. You can get what is with God only through your obedience to Him.

MSH

22

He is not strong who may defeat everyone in a wrestling bout. Mighty is he who controls himself even in a fit of anger.

M/MSH

Aishah, the Prophet's wife, reports that throughout his life the Prophet (peace be upon him) did not take revenge on any personal grounds. He, however, exacted punishment only in a cases involving any violation of God's commands.

B/M

24

The Prophet (peace be upon him) was never seen taking food, while reclining against a pillow or cushion. Nor did he let anyone walk behind him.

D/MSH

Simple living is a sure sign of true faith.

D/M

You cannot be a true believer unless you like for your brother or for your neighbour what you love for yourself.

(M)

If one intends to do a wrong act, God directs angels not to record the same until he actually does it. Once he commits it, only a single evil act is then recorded against him. Conversely, as one intends to do a good deed, yet fails to do so, it is credited to his account as his good act. If he actually performs a good act, he gets a ten-fold reward.

(M)

A true believer is he who practises what he preaches. Moreover, his neighbour should not face any problem from him.

al-Targhib wa al-Tarhib

Virtue consists in your good conduct and evil is that deed which pricks your conscience or that which you would not like others to know.

(M)

Perfection of reason consists in taking steps with far-reaching results, of piety in shunning sins, and of excellent conduct in nobility.

B/M

If you defend the honour of your brother in his absence, by refuting a baseless charge against him, God would certainly protect you from the punishment of Hellfire.

BQ

32

Here is the formula how to endear yourself to God and to men: shun materialism and worldliness, God would love you. Likewise, when you turn indifferent to others' wealth, it would endear you to fellow human beings.

T/I

If you know a truly pious person who does not indulge in vain talk and keeps away from worldliness, you should join his company. God bestows wisdom upon such a pious person.

BQ

34

On deputing Muaz as governor of Yemen, the Prophet (peace be upon him) advised him: "Keep away from the life of luxury. God's chosen servants do not lead a life of ease and comfort."

(A)

35

In both your private and public life you should always fear God. Piety should permeate your conduct. Your good deeds would help in getting your lapses condoned. Treat people well.

A/T

36

The best ones among you are those who have excellent conduct.

B/M

Of all that God has bestowed on man, the most valuable is his good character and conduct.

BQ

Among my Companions, the dearest to me are those who have good conduct.

(B)

They would be denied God's mercy who do not show kindness to others.

B/M

One blessed with true faith cannot fall prey to greed and miserliness. These vices are incompatible with true faith.

(N)

41

A true believer is an embodiment of overflowing love and affection. One who does not love others is devoid of any virtue. He is detested by everyone.

A/BQ

God is All Merciful and He showers leneniency and mercy upon everyone. He grants generously to those who are kind-hearted, not to those who are stern and unrelenting.

(M)

43

Anas, who attended on the Prophet (peace be upon him) for ten years, recounts: "I was a young boy when I started working as his attendant. At times, I did not properly follow his instructions. However, during all these ten years he never rebuked me. Nor did he ever grill my for any of my acts of omission and commission."

(D)

One who refrains from speaking ill of others, God would not disclose his failings. One who controls his anger will be protected from His anger on the Day of Judgement. On who pleads guilty to Him for his sins would be pardoned by Him.

BQ

Saying good, kind words is an act of charity on one's part, which entitles him to God's reward.

(B)

If you pledge to observe the following, I assure you of your entry into Paradise:

(i) Whenever you say something, speak the truth.
(ii) Whenever you promise, keep your word.
(iii) Whenever something is placed under your trust, guard it and return it.
(iv) Do not abuse your private parts.
(v) Avoid even looking at what is forbidden.
(vi) Exercise self-restraint by way of not hurting anyone or depriving him of his due.

A/BQ

One with these three traits is definitely a hypocrite:

(i) He tells a lie whenever he says something.

(ii) He does not keep his word whenever he makes a promise.

(iii) He cheats when something is placed under his trust.

B/M

Wealth does not consist in possessing abundant resources. A contented heart is truly rich.

(B)

If one bears patiently with his loss and suffering in order to please God, he would be admitted to Paradise.

(I)

If one afflicted with distress, be it physical or financial, does not complain, God would grant him Paradise.

Tabarani

God does not look at your faces or your riches. He takes into account only your deeds and your inner-most feelings.

(M)

52

Those dispensing justice fairly would be seated on the pulpits of light, to the right of God. They would be lavishly rewarded for having acted with justice even in cases involving their family and kith and kin.

(M)

O mankind! Listen! Your Lord is One and Adam is everyone's progenitor. No Arab is superior to a non-Arab. Nor is any non-Arab superior to an Arab. No white person is better than a black one. Nor is any black person better than a white one. Your superiority is only the basis of piety.

(A)

54

Do not incur a victim's curse upon you. For his supplication reaches God directly. God does not approve that anyone be oppressed.

MSH

One who knowingly connives with an unjust oppressor stands outside the fold of faith.

MSH

56

Do not speak ill of the dead. They are already with the Lord and would be recompensed for their deeds.

al-Adab al-Mufrad

Follow the middle path. Taking up jobs beyond your capacity would bring only shame upon you.

(T)

Do not be like those who are good only to those who are kind to them. Do not wrong him who wrongs you. You should be kind to even those hostile to you. You should not follow them in their wrongdoing.

MSH

59

One who shares food with his servants, rides a donkey in market and milks his goat bears an excellent conduct, free from the blemish of pride and arrogance.

(M)

60

The following four traits make up excellent character:

(i) Trustworthiness,

(ii) Truthfulness,

(iii) Politeness, and

(iv) Living on lawful earnings.

(T)

Your deliverance or perdition hinge on the following:

(i) Fear of God in both your private and public life.

(ii) Standing by truth whether it suits or harms your interests

(i) Moderation in both adversity and prosperity.

(ii) Getting addicted to base desires

(iii) Overpowering greed and lust

(iv) Self-centredness.

Dismiss the person who praises you to your face.

(M)

63

On being asked whether one's desire for good clothes betrays his inclination towards pride, the Prophet (peace be upon him) replied: "God being the All-Radiant appreciates beauty. Pride, however, consists in looking down upon others and in opposing the truth."

M/MSH

64

One characterized with the following traits will be blessed with peaceful death: i) Leniency towards the weak ii) Love and respect for parents and iii) Taking good care of one's subordinates.

BQ

2. Social Norms and Values

~~~
~~~

If one borrows money with the intention to repay it, yet he is unable to do so, God would enable him to repay it somehow. However, if he did not mean to repay it in the first place, God would destroy him for his evil intention.

(B)

One who gets something from someone should return the favour, if he can afford it. One unable to do so should, at least, praise and thank his benefactor. This too, amounts to repaying the favour done to him. By contrast, one who refuses to acknowledge the favour done to him is an ungrateful wretch.

T/D

One who is not trustworthy is devoid of faith. One who does not keep his word stands outside the fold of faith.

BQ

One should not seek favours from fellow human beings. If one drops something while riding, he should better get off to pick it up, rather than ask someone to do it for him.

69

Faith in Islam guides man to give up all that is vain and trivial.

A/MW

Charity does not decrease one's wealth. Nor does one's humility lower his prestige. If one acts humbly for God's sake, God will certainly exalt him in rank.

(M)

71

One who is not kind-hearted and considerate is not able to perform many good acts.

(M)

One who is not merciful would not be shown any mercy by God.

(M)

Curse be upon him who mutilates animals.

(B)

One who does not publicize someone's lapses would enjoy God's protection on the Day of Judgement. As reward, God would overlook his lapses.

(M)

One consulted for advice should realize the importance of the trust placed in him.

(D)

One who meets the need of a fellow Muslim pleases me. And one who pleases me is rewarded by God with Paradise.

BQ

One taking pains for helping a widow or a poor, needy person is like one who strives in God's way. He is as praiseworthy as one who worships throughout the night, without complaining of fatigue or as one who observes fasts consecutively.

B/M

78

As a Bedouin (a nomadic Arab) visiting a mosque for the first time urinated inside it, those present took to scolding him. The Prophet (peace be upon him), however, intervened, saying: "Leave him alone. Pour some water and wash the floor. You are there to make life easy for everyone. You should not cause hardship to anyone."

(B)

One who curses others himself stands cursed.

(M)

A hypocrite would suffer most in the Afterlife. As he would be consigned to Hell and his entrails would be roasted in Hellfire, the inmates of Hell would gather round him and ask him what had brought such a dreadful punishment on him. For, during his life he used to exhort people to do good and shun evil. In reply he would confess that notwithstanding his preaching, he himself did not practise the same. He committed the very sins against which he used to warn everyone.

(B)

81

He is not a liar who says some kind words of his own in order to bring peace between two quarrelling parties and conveys them such a message, which may draw them closer to each other.

B/M

A generous person gains proximity with God, gets closer to Paradise, and is far removed from Hell. In contrast, a miser is far removed from God and Paradise and moves headlong towards Hell. God loves more a generous person, who may not be very well-versed in religious knowledge, than that miser who is engaged in acts of worship.

(T)

83

Two persons, who were fasting, offered Prayer behind the Prophet (peace be upon him). On noting their indulgence in backbiting, the Prophet (peace be upon him) asked them to repeat their Prayer and to observe fast the next day as expiation for their backbiting.

BQ

84

The expiation for backbiting is that the one guilty of it should earnestly pray to God that his victim be blessed with God's mercy.

Jamey Saghir

One who severs ties of kinship would not gain entry into Paradise.

(D)

There would be a time when the killer would not know as to why he killed someone and his victims would have no idea as to why they were killed.

(M)

87

It is not bigotry to have love for one's own community. Prejudice and unfairness, however, consist in supporting one's community even in their wrong, unjust acts.

A/I

God showers His mercy upon those who are kind and considerate towards fellow human beings.

(B)

89

Whoever among you is capable of helping his/her brother, he/she should do so.

(M)

One who loves God and His Messenger and seeks to win their pleasure, he should

(a) always speak the truth,

(b) justify the trust reposed in him, and

(c) be a good neighbour.

The Prophet (peace be upon him) was informed about a woman who was known for her devotion to prayer, fasting and charity. However, she used to hurt her neighbours with her offensive comments. He dubbed her as an inmate of Hell. On the contrary, he branded another woman as a dweller of Paradise who was kind to her neighbours, though she did not perform any extra Prayer.

A/BQ

He would not be admitted to Paradise, whose neighbours are not safe from his mischief and evil.

(M)

The archangel Gabriel (who brought divine revelation to me) impressed upon me so much the command for treating neighbours well that I thought neighbours would get a share also in inheritance.

(B)

94

God being the Most Compassionate is merciful towards those who show kindness. Be kind to fellow human beings. Your Lord would shower mercy upon you.

D/T

A Muslim owes the following obligations towards fellow Muslims:

(i) He should call on them when they fall ill.

(ii) He should join their funeral.

(iii) He should pay them social visits.

(iv) He should greet them on meeting them.

(v) He should respond to their sneezing, saying "May God have mercy on you."

(vi) He should act sincerely towards them.

(N)

A Muslim who feeds a hungry Muslim would be served with the food of Paradise by God on the Day of Judgment. A Muslim who offers water to a thirsty Muslim would be provided with an excellent sealed drink on the Day of Judgment. A Muslim who clothes a poor Muslim would be dressed in the clothes of Paradise on the Day of Judgement.

(T)

The time spent by one on visiting the sick is credited to his account as the time granted to him for visiting the gardens of Paradise.

(M)

When visiting a sick person the Prophet (peace be upon him) used to tell him: "Do not worry. This would, God willing, compensate for your acts of omission and omission".

(B)

Do you not fear God regarding the animal placed by Him in your custody? Do not keep it hungry or overburden it with hard work.

(M)

To remove from the path what may cause inconvenience to people is also an act of charity.

(B)

101

A widow's marriage had been arranged by her father, without her consent. She did not like her husband. When she approached the Prophet (peace be upon him), he got her marriage annulled.

(B)

102

You should not send your marriage proposal, if another proposal is under consideration. You should go ahead only if that proposal falls through.

B/M

103

Bringing peace between hostile parties is a more blessed act than engaging in Prayers, fasting and charity. By the same token, causing discord in society is something devastatingly destructive.

(D)

104

You should not ask anyone to give his seat to you. Rather, you should make room for each other.

B/M

105

One who takes the lead in greeting others earns greater proximity with God.

A/T

106

The Prophet (peace be upon him) passed by a group of men, including Muslims, Jews and polytheistic idolators, and he greeted all of them with the customary Islamic greeting formula "Peace and blessings be upon you".

B/M

107

One who believes in God and the Day of Judgement, should speak only good. Otherwise, he should maintain silence.

B/M

It does not befit a believer to curse anyone.

(T)

109

Exchange gifts with one another. It puts an end to any ill feeling in your hearts.

(T)

110

One who does not thank his benefactor cannot be grateful to God either.

A/T

111

Avoid speaking ill of the dead. Rather, talk about their virtues and good deeds.

D/T

112

Wealth does not consist in abundant provisions and plenty of resources. A contented person, enjoying peace of mind is a truly rich person.

(B)

113

There is a cure for every disease. A medical remedy suited best for that disease cures one at God's command.

114

Do not take lightly any good deed. It is part of good manners to receive your brother or friend warmly. Same holds true for doing them a favour, no matter how small it might be.

(T)

115

On coming to know someone's misdeed, the Prophet (peace be upon him) did not name the culprit in his sermon. Rather, he warned people against the evil of that misdeed in general terms.

(D)

116

On being asked how many times one should pardon his servant, the Prophet (peace be upon him) replied. "Overlook his lapses seventy times a day."

(T)

117

A perfect believer is he who does not hurt anyone with his tongue or hands.

(B)

118

A guardian of an orphan and I would be so close to each other in Paradise, as my two fingers are.

(M)

119

He is not a believer, whose neighbour is not safe from his mischief and evil.

(M)

120

It is not becoming of a believer to go to bed after having a full meal while his neighbour may have nothing to eat.

MSH

121

The first directive in the morning by the Prophet's Companions to their family members was to feed the orphan and to take good care of him.

Sahifa al-Haq

122

Help your brother, be he the victim or the oppressor. Helping the oppressor stands for dissuading him from doing injustice to anyone.

M/MSH

123

Shun suspicion and conjecture. Suspicions is premised on falsehood.

MSH

124

One who believes in God and the Hereafter should either speak good words or keep quiet. Moreover, he should be kind to his neighbours and extend hospitality to his guests.

(M)

125

If you want large sustenance and a long, ripe age, you should maintain well the ties of kinship.

B/M

126

If you seek wealth, while using fair means, for becoming financially independent, for supporting your family and for helping your neighbours, you would be raised on the Day of Judgement, with your face shining as bright as the full moon. However, if you are after only worldly glory and amass wealth in order to make a show and to earn people's praise, you would face God's wrath on the Day of Judgement.

BQ

127

Make the most while you are in the following states:

(i) Youth before you turn old.

(ii) Prosperity before you are afflicted with adversity.

(iii) Leisure time before you are overwhelmed with work.

(iv) Health before you fall ill.

(v) Life before you breathe your last.

(T)

128

God commands that man's conduct should be characterized by the following traits:

(i) Fearing God in both his private and public life.

(ii) Adhering to justice, no matter whether he is friendly or hostile to the parties concerned.

(iii) Following the middle path in both prosperity and adversity.

(iv) Maintaining ties of kinship even with those relatives

who sever these ties and misbehave.

(v) Kindness towards even those who act unjustly to him, depriving him of his due.

(vi) Forgiving those who offended and oppressed him

(vii) Reflecting on the divine signs around him and on his relationship with God in terms of taking stock of his conduct.

(viii) Remembering God constantly by way of saying and doing what God has commanded

(ix) Drawing lessons from everything and enjoining people to do good.

Razin

129

On coming to know that one of his Companions, Uthman ibn Mazun had turned into an almost ascetic, having renounced his family life and was engaged day and night only in acts of worship the Prophet (peace be upon him) sent for him and asked him to follow his way, saying: "Look here. I sleep for a few hours at night and offer early morning Prayer as well. I do keep fasts yet not everyday. I marry women and maintain my relations with them. You should fear God and not neglect the obligations which you owe to your family, your body and your guests. Your children have their rights on you. So do your body and your guests have their rights on you. Keep fast yet take food as well. Offer Prayers as well as sleep at night.

(D)

Islam does not allow celibacy.

(D)

131

Do not delay the following:

(i) Pray as soon as it is time for Prayer.

(ii) Bury your dead as soon as coffin is ready.

(iii) Marry your daughter as soon as you find a suitable match for her.

(T)

132

The best Muslim home is the one that houses an orphan and who is looked after properly. Conversely, the worst one is that in which he/she is maltreated.

I/A

133

Of all the permitted acts, divorce is the most detestable one in the sight of God.

(D)

134

Before entering someone's house, seek permission. You should return, if permission is not granted.

(D)

135

O servants of God! Be brethren to one another. All believers are part of the same fraternity.

A believer does not wrong the other one. Nor does he leave him in the lurch.

(i) Do not look down upon others.

(ii) Do not be jealous of one another.

(iii) Do not nurse any grudge against others.

(iv) Do not sever mutual ties.

(v) Do not provoke hostility among one another.

All this constitutes piety. Evil is he who humiliates a fellow believer. The life, property and honour of a believer are sacred for all other believers.

(M)

136

One who harms others would be harmed by God. One who is hostile towards others, God would afflict him with hardship.

(T)

137

As one proceeds to call on a sick person, he is enveloped by God's mercy. As long as he stays with the sick, he is rewarded with God's mercy.

MSH

138

He is not a believer who has square meal whereas his neighbour starves.

(I)

139

Beware! I warn you strongly regarding your obligations towards the weak, especially the rights of orphans and women.

Riyad al-Salihin

140

Blessed is that wedding that does not entail any financial burden.

BQ

141

One joining a gathering should not disturb those already seated. Rather, they should cheerfully make room for him.

(A)

142

That wife can never enter Paradise who seeks separation from her husband, without a very pressing, valid reason.

A/T

143

O God! Let not a wicked person do me a favour which I may have to repay in this world or in the Next One.

Kanz al-Ummal

144

Do not be eager to have an encounter with your enemy. Rather, seek God's safety and protection. However, once war is declared, be consistent and steadfast in fighting against the enemy.

B/M

One who declines invitation to meal, without a valid reason, is guilty of having disobeyed God and His Messenger. By contrast, an uninvited person who gatecrashes into a feast is as wicked as a burglar or robber.

D/*MSH*

146

Avoid urinating or defecating at i) river side ii) road side and iii) under a shady tree.

D/*MSH*

147

Man should not hate his wife in view of something in her which he dislikes. She may have other traits which are pleasing.

M/*MSH*

148

Your neighbours are the best judge of your conduct. If they speak highly of you, you are blessed with good morals and manners. If they speak ill of you, it is a pointer to your bad conduct.

I/*MSH*

149

The community does not attain piety that does not take good care of the weak and the poor.

MSH

150

If you lead Prayer, think of your congregation i.e. the old and the weak standing behind you. Therefore do not prolong Prayer. However, when praying singly, you may prolong your Prayer as much as you like.

B/M

151

As your servant prepares food for you, he does a painstaking, toilsome job. You are obliged to seat him beside you at meal.

M/*Mishkat*

152

All the believers constitute a single fraternity. They do not betray, cheat or wrong one another. Rather, each believer holds out a mirror to another, in alerting him to his lapses.

T/ *MSH*

153

Believers are like a structure, of which every part is inseparably joined with another. They should help one another when in distress.

MSH

154

If you take advice from others before taking an important step, you would not regret your decision later. Likewise, if you always follow the middle path, marked by moderation and prudence, you would not end up as a pauper.

al-Mujam al-Saghir

One who defends a fellow believer in his absence while he is reviled, God would deliver him from Hellfire.

BQ

156

A true worshipper believes in the essential goodness of others.

A/*MSH*

157

You must secure permission before entering the house of even your own children, parents, brother or sister.

al-Adab al-Mufrad

158

Your pious friend is like a bearer of musk. You would be, at least, blessed with fragrance in his company. As opposed to it, your wicked, evildoing friend is like an ironsmith at work. His company is bound to pollute you.

MSH

159

If you do not accept the apology offered by a fellow Muslim, you would incur God's punishment for your hard-heartedness.

BQ/*MSH*

160

I fear the appearance of such eloquent persons in your midst whose sayings would be marked be profoundness and high morals yet their deeds would reek of evil and wickedness.

BQ/*MSH*

161

If you wrong or overburden your allies or usurp what rightfully belongs to them, I would fight their case against you on the Day of Judgement.

(D)

162

If three of you are travelling together, you should take one of you as leader to oversee all the arrangements.

(D)

3. Major Sins

163

If one fails to defend a fellow Muslim's honour which is under attack, despite his ability to do so, he would be punished by God in both this life and the Next Life.

Sharah al-Sunnah

164

One who asks people to keep standing while attending on him and enjoys it reserves a place for himself in Hell.

T/D

165

The worst person is he whom people avoid in view of his bad manners. God would deal harshly with him on the Day of Judgement.

(D)

166

I say it with all the force at my command that usurping the rights of these two weak sections of society—orphans and women—is a major sin.

(N)

167

Two of you should not whisper to each other in the presence of the third one. For it would offend him.

(M)

On being asked what one should dread most, the Prophet (peace be upon him), pointed to the tongue, asserting that one should be very careful about what he says lest it might incur sins.

(T)

169

The following types of persons would not be admitted to Paradise:

(i) Those who cheat people,

(ii) Those who are miserly, and

(iii) Those who remind people of their favours.

Tuhfa al-Ahwazi

Taking back one's gift is as odious as a dog licking its own vomit.

B/MSH

171

One who has even an ioata of pride in his heart cannot enter Paradise. By the same token, one who has an iota of faith would not be hurled into Hell.

(M)

172

Be on your guard against the menacing vice of jealousy. It wipes out one's good deeds as rapidly as fire destroys wood.

(D)

173

Do not rejoice at some calamity befalling another person. For, God might relieve him and afflict you with the same.

(T)

174

Someone requested the Prophet (peace be upon him) to give him some advice. He advised him: "Do not lose temper." When he sought another piece of advice, the Prophet (peace be upon him) repeated the same: "Do not lose temper."

(B)

175

A true believer is he who does not vilify or curse anyone. Nor does he utter obscene, abusive words.

(T)

176

A true believer cannot reconcile with cheating and falsehood.

A/BQ

177

One who usurps someone's belongings by taking a false oath would appear as a leper before God on the Day of Judgment.

(D)

178

On the death of his Companion, Muaz's son, the Prophet (peace be upon him) sent him the following note of condolence.

In the name of God, Most Compassionate, Most Merciful: All praise be to God, besides Whom there is no god. I pray to God to shower His rewards upon you for the loss you have suffered. May He grant you peace of mind and heart. May He enable us and you to thank Him for His numerous blessings. The truth is that our lives, our belongings and our family members are precious gifts from Him. Rather, these are trusts placed with us. Your son too, was one of His blessings granted to you. As long as it pleased Him, He let you enjoy it. As He willed, He recalled it. You are nonetheless destined to receive a big reward for this loss. I give you the glad tidings of His special mercy, if your bear patiently with this loss in order to earn His pleasure and reward.

O Muaz! Be patient lest your lamentation might not wipe out your reward. It would render you all the more regretful and poorer. Remember that your mourning cannot bring back the dead. Nor can it relieve your loss and suffering. God's command is bound to prevail. His will has already been accomplished. Peace and blessing upon you!

Mu'jam Kabir

179

The following are some of the major sins:

(i) To associate anyone with God in His divinity.

(ii) To disobey parents.

(iii) To kill anyone.

(iv) To tell a lie.

(M)

180

Accursed are both—one who bribes and one who accepts it.

D/T

181

One who lays a false claim to something which is not his is not a believer. Such dishonesty would land him into Hell.

(M)

182

One who usurps someone's belonging, even it be a twig, by taking a false oath cannot enter Paradise. God has ordained Hell for him.

(M)

183

Once addressing his followers, the Prophet (peace be upon him) cautioned them. "I am a human being like you. You refer disputes to me for judgment. The more articulate one may persuade me to decide the case in his favour. If I ever do so, do not go by my judgement. For, what I might award you on the basis of your false oath would take you straight to Hell."

B/M

184

Whereas God may defer punishment for one's other sins until the Day of Recompense, one guilty of denying his parents their due and disobeying them is punished in this world itself. This is in addition to the punishment which would be inflicted upon him in the Hereafter.

BQ

One who lusts for name and fame would be disgraced by God on the Day of Judgement.

D/*MSH*

186

You would be held a liar if you report what you heard, without verifying that report.

M/*MSH*

187

A die-hard hypocrite is one who always i) betrays the trust reposed in him, ii) resorts to telling lies, iii) fails to keep his word and iv) uses filthy, abusive language in a quarrel.

Beware! If you have even one of the above traits, you would be reckoned as a hypocrite.

MSH

188

Return even the needle and thread which you may have borrowed from someone. Your breach of trusts would bring disgrace upon you on the Day of Judgement.

N/*MSH*

4. Beliefs and Practices

189

He is a true believer who feels gratified on doing something good and is overcome with sorrow and remorse on doing anything evil.

al-Mustadrak

190

If one retires to bed with the intention to get up the next morning for offering the early morning Prayer yet fails to do so as he oversleeps, he would be still credited with having performed that Prayer. His oversleeping would be condoned by the Lord out of His grace and affection.

N/I

191

One who travels in pursuit of knowledge is like he who proceeds towards Paradise. Angels spread their wings, welcoming the seeker of knowledge. All those in the heavens and on earth, including even the fish inside deep waters pray and seek forgiveness for him. A scholar enjoys such superiority over a worshipper which the full moon has over the stars.

(D)

192

If you are in doubt about the propriety of an act, do not do it. Rather, you should do only what you know to be good. Truth blesses you with the peace of mind whereas falsehood torments you with uneasiness and tension

T/N

193

A believer perceives his misdeeds as a rock that is about to crush him whereas a wicked person dismisses his sins like shooing a fly around him.

(B)

194

O people! Seek God's forgiveness. I turn in repentance to Him one hundred times a day.

(M)

195

Every human being is liable to committing lapses. However, the best one is he who repents his lapse.

T/I

One who constantly seeks God's forgiveness is shown a way out. God helps him surmount every hardship and relieves him from every worry and sorrow. He provides him with sustenance from unexpected quarters.

A/D/I

197

At the time of the creation of the universe, God proclaimed: "My mercy exceeds far more than My anger."

B/M/T

The best worshipper is he who looks forward to excellent recompense from his Lord.

A/D

199

One who wants to be fully protected from Hell and is keen on entering Paradise should breathe his last in the state of faith, with belief in God and the Day of Judgement. He should behave with people in the same good manner as he wants them to treat him.

(M)

200

On being asked to curse the polytheists persecuting him, the Prophet (peace by upon him) declared: "I have not been sent down in order to curse people. Rather, I have come as mercy unto the world."

(M)

201

Do not be immoderate in praising me. Do not be like Christians who have gone too far in extolling Jesus, son of Mary. I am merely a servant of God. Regard me only as a servant and Messenger of God.

B/M

202

No one can enter Paradise by dint of his deeds alone. May God envelope us in His mercy and affection. Follow the way of faith steadfastly. Do not wish for death. For, if you are good, you should better repent as long as you are alive, which would please God.

(B)

203

Whenever some good news reached the Prophet (peace be upon him), he used to fall into prostration for giving thanks to God.

(B)

204

As a girl appeared before the Prophet (peace be upon him), he told her: "When a girl comes of age, she should keep her body covered. You may, however, keep your face and hands open".

(M)

205

There are some couplets which do abound in wisdom.

B/M

206

Labid [an Arab poet of the Prophet's day] articulated profound truth in his couplet: "Beware! Everyone other than God is false and mortal."

B/M

207

Remember God, He would remember you. Keep mentioning God, you would find Him around you. Seek whatever you need only from Him. Whenever you are in distress, invoke only Him for rescue. Even if all human beings together want to help you, they cannot do so. You would get only what God has ordained for you. Likewise, if all of them intend to harm you, they cannot, except what God has already decreed for you.

MSH

208

The human heart, like iron, is liable to turn rusty. Remembrance of death and recitation of the Quran protects the heart from getting tarnished.

MSH

209

One engaged in remembering God is a truly alive person. By contrast, one who disregards his Lord is like a dead person.

B/M

210

"O Quraysh [my tribesmen]! Take steps to protect yourselves from Hellfire. I cannot release you from God's grip. O family members of Abd Manaf [my family]! I cannot avert divine punishment from you. O Abbas [my uncle]! I cannot be of any help to you on the Day of Judgement. O Safia [my aunt]! I cannot delay divine punishment for you even by a second. O my daughter, Fatima! I can give you as much of my wealth as I like. However, I cannot keep divine punishment away from you. So all of you should strive for your deliverance. Your faith and good deeds alone would help you in the Afterlife.

B/M

211

He who is blessed with the following would enjoy the best of both the worlds:

(i) A heart overflowing with thankfulness to God,

(ii) A tongue engaged consistently in the remembrance of God,

(iii) A temperament to tolerate loss and suffering, and

(iv) A sincere and loyal wife.

BQ/MSH

212

A single religious scholar gifted with understanding and tact is far more effective in thwarting Satan's mischief than a large number of devout, naïve worshippers.

T/MSH

213

The Prophet (peace be upon him) asked those sitting beside him: "Do you think there would be any impurity or dirt on the body of one who takes bath five times a day in a lake flowing in front of his house?" When they emphatically ruled it out, he asserted: "My parable alludes to the five obligatory Prayers a day. God condones one's lapses as reward for his regularly offering five daily Prayers."

(B)

214

Avoid minor sins as well. God would hold your accountable for these, too.

I/MSH

215

If you repose trust in God in a befitting manner, He would grant you sustenance in the same manner as He feeds birds. Birds leave their nests at dawn on empty stomach and return at dusk with their bellies full.

T/MSH

216

Such are the chosen servants of God that on meeting them one instinctively remembers God. And the worst of His servants are those who sow discord among people and falsely implicate the innocent.

A/BQ

217

You are not superior to any black or white person. You can excel others only by dint of your piety.

(A)

218

Lead your life in this world as a traveler who is on his way.

(B)

219

God offered me to have abundant wealth. Valleys of Makkah overflowing with gold were presented before me. However, I submitted to Him: “I do not seek wealth. Rather, I prefer to eat one day and to sleep on an empty stomach the next day. For in this case, on feeling hungry, I would turn more fervently to You and invoke You humbly. And when blessed with food, I would grow more grateful to You.”

A/T

220

God has provided cure for every disease.

(B)

221

All creatures are part of God's family. God loves him most who is kind to His creatures.

MSH

222

Even if part of one's income is unlawful, his Prayer is not accepted by God.

(A)

223

The flesh or body fed on unlawful earnings is unfit for Paradise. This is suited only for Hellfire.

A/BQ

224

The smell from the mouth of a fasting person is more agreeable to God than the fragrance of musk.

(M)

225

Pay Zakah on your wealth. For it is truly a purifier that cleanses you. Be kind to your kith and kin and fulfil the rights of the poor, neighbours and beggars.

(M)

226

Prayer is the joy of my eyes.

B/M

227

When a sinner turns to God in repentance, it pleases Him as much as a traveler in a desert is delighted to get back his lost camel.

B/M

228

God accepts man's repentance even when he is on the verge of death.

(T)

229

Someone asked the Prophet (peace be upon him) whether he should tie his camel or let it loose, entrusting it to God's care. He directed him to tie it first securely and then entrust it to God's protection.

(T)

230

Do not be vie with those who are better off than you. It would help you appreciate all the more what God has granted you.

(M)

231

One is influenced much by the company he keeps. Before your enter into friendship with someone, find out about his beliefs and practices.

A/*MSH*

Section II

How to lead life together

5. Family Life

~~~
~~~

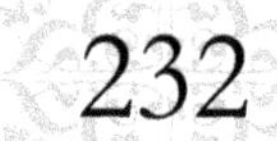

On being blessed with a child, parents should first give him/her a good name and ensure his/her moral upbringing. As he/she comes of age, they should arrange for his/her marriage. Otherwise, they would be accountable, if he/she indulges in unlawful sex.

BQ

233

Accursed is he who has anal sex with his wife.

On being asked whether a Muslim may maintain ties with his/her non-Muslim mother, the Prophet (peace be upon him) replied: "Yes, you should fulfil your obligations towards her and treat her well."

(M)

235

One who wants that his sustenance be enlarged and that he may enjoy a long life, he should treat well his kith and kin and do favours to them.

B/M

236

One guilty of severing the ties of kinship will not be admitted to Paradise.

B/M

237

Someone sought the Prophet's permission to join *Jihad* (fighting in God's way). He asked him whether his mother was alive. As he affirmed it, he directed him to stay at home and take care of her. The Prophet (peace be upon him) concluded his directive thus: "Go and look after her. Paradise lies at the feet of your mother."

A/N/BQ

238

Treat your children with kindness and affection. Arrange for their moral upbringing.

(I)

239

As one dies, his record of deeds is sealed. However, for the following three deeds of his, he continues earning God's reward, even after his death:

(i) His endowment for some charitable work.

(ii) His leaving behind such scholarly works which may be used profitably by subsequent generations.

(iii) His virtuous children who may pray for him.

240

After the death of your father you should maintain social relations with his friends. This constitutes a good act and courtesy on your part.

(M)

241

What you eat, and what you feed to your wife, your children and your servants constitute an act of charity.

al-Adab al-Mufrad

You may serve and please your parents, even after their death by

(i) Praying for their forgiveness and deliverance,

(ii) Honouring the commitments made by them,

(iii) Treating well their friends, and

(iv) Maintaining their ties of kinship

al-Adab al-Mufrad

243

As a baby girl is born in a family, God deputes angels there, who proclaim: "O members of this family! Blessings be upon you" Then they take the baby girl under their wings, stroke her hair and say: "Here is a weak, helpless being. One who brings her up would enjoy God's support until the Last Day."

Tabarani

244

If one's parents die and he/she was unable to serve them properly, all is not lost. He/she should consistently seek God's forgiveness for the deceased parents. On the Day of Judgment he/she would be reckoned as their devoted, obedient child.

BQ

245

Generally people select their prospective wives on the following considerations: her wealth, her noble family background and her beauty. You should, however, choose only a devout marriage partner, giving priority only to her religious mindset.

(B)

246

Of all the commitments your make, the most serious one, which should be promptly fulfilled, is the payment of dower to your wife. It is dower which sanctifies your sexual relations with her.

B/M

247

That marriage feast is detestable, to which only the rich are invited while leaving out the poor.

B/M

The best one among you is he who is kind to his wife and children. I am its role model.

(M)

249

A perfect believer is he who is of excellent conduct. The best ones among you are those who treat their wives well.

(B)

250

Aishah, the Prophet's wife is on record reporting that the Prophet (peace be upon him) used to assist her in domestic chores.

(B)

251

That wife would enter Paradise, with whom her husband was happy until his death.

(N)

Of all the worldly bounties, the most valuable one is a good wife.

M/N

253

Respect your children and provide them with the best moral instruction.

(I)

That father who does not bury alive her daughter, who does not degrade her and who does not prefer her to his son would be admitted to Paradise.

(D)

255

One who brings up three daughters, instructs them well in morals and manners, gets them married and treats them well would get a place in Paradise.

(D)

256

When Asma, a female Companion, sought the Prophet's ruling how she should treat her unbelieving mother, who was on a visit to her, he told her to take good care of her unbelieving mother and to offer her financial help, if she needed it.

(B)

257

God may pardon any sin. However, He has decreed that one guilty of disobedience to parents would face punishment in this world itself.

MSH

258

He who acts kindly towards those relatives who are good to him does not do justice to the ties of kinship in its real sense. Rather, he discharges this obligation perfectly who maintains ties of kinship with even those who sever relationship.

(B)

259

A dutiful, loving son who only looks at his parents with love and kindness will earn the reward awarded for doing Hajj (Pilgrimage) for each glance of his. Even if he casts such a glance one hundred times a day, he would be credited with the same reward for each glance. Almighty God's treasure is not diminished on account of such generous and lavish rewards.

BQ

260

A good wife is man's most precious asset in this world.

(M)

261

Once someone came to the Prophet (peace be upon him), crying profusely over a major sin committed by him and asked how he should atone for it. The latter asked him whether his parents were alive. As he replied in the negative, the Prophet (peace be upon him) directed him to serve and take good care of his maternal aunt.

(T)

262

The best thing which parents can give to their children is their excellent moral upbringing and training.

MSH

263

Your best charity is the one given to those dependent upon you.

D/*MSH*

6. Economic Life

264

Spend your wealth; do not keep counting it. Otherwise, God would grant you in a restricted measure. Do not be miserly. Otherwise, God would not grant you in an abundant measure. Donate as much as you can.

B/M

265

Eat, drink, dress yourselves and give in charity as long as it does not border on extravagance or show-off.

A/N

266

You should better pick wood in a forest and sell it for getting bread. It is far better for you than begging for food.

I/A

267

A Muslim who plants a tree or is engaged in farming is rewarded for doing charity, as humans and other living beings eat of his produce, even if he does not give it willingly to them.

M/A

268

God loves that believer who works hard to earn his bread:

Tabarani

269

The best earning is a worker's income, provided that he works honestly and sincerely.

(A)

270

On being asked to specify the best means of income, the Prophet (peace be upon him) spelled out the following: "Manual work and fair trading."

MSH

271

While selling your goods, do not take recourse to false, misleading oaths. This might boost your business for a while. However, in the long run, you would not attain prosperity.

(M)

272

A trader guilty of hoarding is a sinner.

al-Muntaqa

273

A trader not resorting to hoarding earns God's mercy whereas the one guilty of it stands cursed.

(I)

274

It is not lawful for a trader to sell an item, without pointing to its defect, if any. If he knows it to be defective, he is obliged to bring it to the customer's notice.

al-Muntaqa

275

God would show mercy to him who is lenient and polite in his business transactions, especially in demanding the repayment of his loan.

(B)

276

There would come a time when people would turn wholly indifferent to the issue whether their income is lawful or not.

(B)

Once while the Prophet (peace be upon him) was seated along with his Companions, a labourer passed by. Those present commented that if his toil had been in God's cause, it would have been much better. The Prophet (peace be upon him), however, corrected them, saying: "If his efforts are geared towards supporting his children, he is still working in God's cause. Same holds true, if his objective is to provide sustenance for his parents. Even if his striving aims at earning some income which would save him from begging others, he is working in God's way. Only if his motive is to make a show of his wealth, he is following in Satan's footsteps."

(B)

278

If you grant relief to the borrower, God would be lenient towards you on the Day of Recompense.

M/MSH

279

God would show mercy to him who acts with generosity and leniency in his business transactions and in demanding his due.

B/MSH

280

God loves His self-respecting servant who, though poor, avoids begging from others.

(I)

281

Strive for earning your bread lawfully. It is one of your most important duties.

BQ

282

Blessed is he who does some manual work for earning his bread. God's Messenger, Prophet David did manual labour for his livelihood.

(B)

283

One who plants orchards or plants or does farming is credited with having performed an act of charity, as men, birds and animals eat their produce.

B/M

284

If one gives some money in charity out of his unlawful earnings, God does not accept it. Nor does He bless such income. One guilty of getting money unlawfully is destined for Hell.

(A)

285

One who sells something defective, without alerting the buyer to it, incurs God's wrath and angels keep cursing and reproaching him.

(I)

286

Pay a worker his wages promptly, even before he stops perspiring.

(I)

287

Keep exchanging presents among you. It removes any ill feeling which you may have for one another.

(T)

288

If one recommends someone's case and accepts a gift in return, he commits a sinister evil act.

(D)

289

One may devote his whole life to acts of worship and lead life in strict obedience to God yet he may end up in Hell for having denied his heirs their due, by leaving behind an unfair bequest.

T/D

290

A worker's wages represent the best income, provided that he does his job sincerely and diligently.

(A)

291

One who deprives his heir of his share in inheritance would be denied any share in Paradise.

(I)

292

God forgives every sin of a martyr, except the uncleared loan which he had taken from someone.

(M)

293

God blesses business partners as long as they are honest and sincere to each other. However, as one of them starts cheating the other, God withdraws His blessings from them.

(D)

One who hoards grain is a sinner.

M/*MSH*

7. Political Life

295

In an Islamic state Muslims pledge to protect the lives, belongings and honour of all the non-Muslim citizens. If anyone wrongs them, deprives them of their rights, oppresses them or usurps their belongings, I would take up these victims' case at God's court.

(D)

296

You may protect yourselves against God's wrath befalling you, provided you kindly treat inarticulate, dumb animals. Ride them only as long as they are fit. Give them proper rest at the end of a journey.

(D)

297

A woman of the influential Banu Makhzum tribe committed theft. Her tribesmen asked Usama, who was very close to the Prophet (peace be upon him), to drop kind words about her so that she might be spared the punishment prescribed by Islamic law. A he recommended her case, the Prophet (peace be upon him) chided him for perverting the course of justice. Immediately he summoned a public meeting in which he delivered the following address: "O people! Earlier communities had faced divine punishment on this very count that they used to enforce penal code only on the weak and the poor while the powerful among them got away with their crimes. By God, even if my daughter, Fatima commits theft, I would impose on her the punishment ordained by Islamic law."

B/M

298

One who blindly supports the unjust action of his family, tribe or community follows the path of self-destruction.

(D)

299

If you extirpate an evil in your society, God would spare you. Same holds true for him who protests against it, if it is beyond his capacity to remove it. Even he who resents it in the heart of his heart would not be taken to task by God in that he was not in a position to extirpate or denounce it. However, mere detestation of evil represents the weakest degree of one's faith.

(N)

300

It is binding upon you to obey your ruler, whether you like his commands or not. You are not, however, obliged to follow him if he asks you to defy any of the divine commandments.

MSH

301

A ruler who does not take good care of his subjects would be dragged on the Day of Judgement by his face and hurled into Hell.

al-Mujam al-Saghir

302

That ruler who causes hardship to the public would be harshly punished by God. On the contrary, one who is kind and affectionate to his subjects would be blessed with God's mercy in the Hereafter.

(M)

303

If a ruler does not protect the interests of my community in the same way as he takes care of his own family, he would be denied entry into Paradise.

al-Mujam al-Saghir

304

Do not run after an office. If you do so, you would be lost in discharging your duty. However, if an office is assigned to you, God would help and support you.

B/M

305

People get only such rulers who befit them.

MSH

306

Judges are of three kinds:

(i) Those who honestly decide cases would have Paradise as their abode.

(ii) Those who dishonestly decide cases would end up in Hell.

(iii) Those who decide cases non-seriously, without ascertaining truth, would also be consigned to Hell.

D/I

307

Punish alike those who are your kin and those who are not. Do not be cowed down by anyone's criticism in enforcing justice in accordance with God's commands.

I/*MSH*

Section III

8. The After Life

308

Murder cases will be the first to be taken up on the Day of Reckoning.

B/M

309

Everyone would have to answer the following five questions on the Day of Judgement:

(i) How did he lead his life?

(ii) How far did he act on the religious knowledge which he had gained?

(iii) How did he earn his wealth?

(iv) How did he spend his wealth?

(v) What did preoccupy him in life?

(T)

310

By God, if you come to know in full about God's wrath and the dreadful scenes of the Day of Judgment, which are in my knowledge, you would cry profusely and cease laughing.

(B)

The wisest one among you is he who is ever-conscious of his death and prepares himself for it. He gains the best of both the worlds in that he is honoured in life and would be warmly received in the Hereafter.

Tabarani

312

On the Day of Judgement God would instruct angels to keep those away from Hell who had ever remembered or feared Him in this world.

T/BQ

313

Whoever does not abuse his tongue and his private parts is guarnteed to enter Paradise.

(B)

314

One who carries tales cannot enter Paradise.

B/M

315

Do not indulge in backbiting. Nor should you spy on or publicize others' failings. Whoever is guilty of it would be treated likewise by God. And he is bound is to be disgraced publicly.

(D)

316

The Prophet (peace be upon him) defined backbiting thus: "Speaking of someone is such terms which might offend him." Someone queried whether mentioning one's failings amounted to backbiting. The Prophet (peace be upon him) affirmed: "This is what backbiting is. Otherwise, if you ascribe to him a failing which he does not have, it constitutes slandering him, which is a more heinous sin than backbiting."

(M)

317

An honest, trustworthy businessman would enjoy the privileged company of God's Messengers, the truthful ones and martyrs in the Next Life.

(T)

318

He would end up as an utter loser in the Next Life, who violates the code of morals and justice in order to help someone unlawfully. So doing, he courts his own loss in the Hereafter.

MSH

319

On the Day of Judgement one would enjoy shade and comfort as a reward for his charitable deeds

(A)

320

Keep visiting graveyard. It is the most effective reminder of the Hereafter.

I/*MSH*

321

The way to Paradise is marked by self-restraint whereas the gratification of the base desires of the self drives one straight to Hell.

MSH

322

Those of you who have an excellent conduct would enjoy my company. On the contrary, those with ill-manners and sharp, reproaching tongues would be kept away from me.

BQ/*MSH*

323

On observing someone using a lot of water for ablution, the Prophet (peace be upon him) censured him. He asked him not to waste a drop of water ever when he is beside a river.

A/*MSH*

324

The following evils would be rampant before the end of the world, i.e. the Last Day:

(i) Only the elite would be greeted whereas the commoners would be neglected with contempt.

(ii) Such craze for amassing wealth and a higher standard of life that wives would be full-time business partners of their husbands.

(iii) Ties of kinship would be disregarded altogether.

(iv) Explosion of knowledge

(v) False testimony would be fairly common, as no one would come forward to testify to the truth.

al-Adab al-Mufrad

325

You would soon lust for power, coveting worldly offices. This would, however, bring only disgrace upon you on the Day of Judgement.

(D)

Section IV

9. Supplications

326

O God! I seek Your refuge from that knowledge which is not beneficial, from that supplication which goes unanswered, from that heart that does not fear You, and from the self that is never satiated.

(I)

327

O God! I earnestly seek from You beneficial knowledge, deeds acceptable to You, and lawful, wholesome sustenance.

I/A

328

While drinking water, do not gulp it down in one go. Rather, take sips (small mouthfuls). As you start drinking, say: “In the name of God, Most Compassionate, Most Merciful”, and when you finish, say: “Praise be to God”.

(T)

329

When you finish eating and drinking, say: "Praise be to God Who provided us with food and drink and made us believers."

T/D

330

O*n retiring to bed*: "O God! I live and die in Your name."

On getting up: "All praise and thanks be to God Who revived me. To Him is the return when we would be resurrected after death."

(M)

331

When you sneeze, you should say: "Praise be to God." Those present around you should respond, saying: "May God have mercy on you". In return, that person should offer this supplication: "May God grant you guidance and improve your affairs."

(B)

332

On visiting the sick, the Prophet (peace be upon him) used to bless him with this supplication: "O Lord! Remove his/her suffering. You alone can grant cure. Bestow such cure which may eliminate his/her disease altogether."

(M)

On the Day of Judgement, the earth would testify to all the deeds of every man and woman, presenting an accurate record of every happening.

Tuhfa al-Ahwazi

334

While all other human beings would be roasting in the scorching heat on the Day of Judgement, the following persons would be seated on the Day of Judgment beneath God's throne, enjoying shade and comfort:

(i) A fair and just ruler.

(ii) The youth who spent his time on acts of worship.

(iii) He who was keen on visiting mosque for offering Prayers.

(iv) He who loved and met others only for God's sake

(v) He who was seduced by a woman of beauty and rank yet he spurned her out of the fear of God.

(vi) He who gave in charity secretly, without bringing it to anyone's knowledge

(vii) He who remembered God in private and cried out of the fear of God.

(B)

335

O Lord! I seek Your refuge against hardship, sorrow, inaction and laziness, burden of debt and influence of evil persons.

B/M

On being faced with loss and suffering one should not wish for death. Unable to bear with pain one may, at most, offer the following supplication: "O Lord! Keep me alive as long as it is good for me and cause me to die when it is better for me."

B/MSH

337

O Lord! Bless me with the best conduct. You alone can instruct me in this. Help me shed all that is bad in my conduct. Only You can enable me to do so.

(M)

338

On visiting the sick: "O Lord of men! Relieve him of his pain and suffering. Grant him full recovery, free from every disease. Only You can grant cure. No one other than You can cure him."

(M)

339

O Lord! Grant us increase and do not afflict us with decrease. Exalt us and do not abase us. Bestow bounties upon us and do not deprive us.

B/M

340

O God! We seek from You ways and means to attain forgiveness, deliverance and protection from all sins. We seek from You abundance of good, entry into Paradise and protection from Hellfire.

Kanz al-Ummal

341

O God! I seek from You beneficial knowledge.

BQ

342

O God! Forgive my sins, both inadvertent and deliberate ones.

(B)

343

O God! You cause the hearts to incline towards something. So incline our hearts towards obeying You.

(M)

344

O God! I seek Your protection from cowardice, lethargy and laziness. I seek Your refuge against excessively old age, debt, Hellfire and punishment in Hell, torment and punishment of the grave, the evil of both affluence and poverty, and against hard-heartedness, negligence, lack of resources, humiliation and helplessness.

I seek Your refuge against unbelief, obstinacy, showing off, deafness, dumbness, madness, leprosy and all tormenting diseases. I seek Your protection against the burden of debt, worries, sorrows, miserliness, others lording over me and over-ripe old age.

(I)

345

O God! Increase my sustenance in my old age and at the end of my life.

Mustadrak

346

O God! Bless me with patience and gratitude. Humble me in my own eyes while exalt me in the eyes of others.

Kanz al-Ummal

347

O God! Bless our country with abundance, prosperity and peace. Do not deprive me of the fruits of what You have granted me. Do not put me to a trial regarding what You have not granted me.

Kanz al-Ummal

348

O God! You have created me in the best mould. Make my conduct equally excellent. Remove from my heart all ill feelings and protect me until my death against the lure of those who misguide.

(A)

O God! Help me lead life as a humble person and cause my death in the state of humility. Include me among the humble ones.

Kitab al-Adhkar

350

O God! Make me one of those who are pleased with doing something good and who seek Your forgiveness as soon as they do something wrong.

(I)

As a believer makes a supplication to God, it is granted in one of the following three ways:

(i) It is fulfilled in this life.

(ii) Or he would be recompensed in the Next Life

(iii) Or it helps avert some calamity befalling him.

(A)

352

F*or a newly-wedded couple:* May God bless you, lavish His bounties on you and keep you together in all that is good and blessed.

A/*MSH*

353

What should we say when we leave house: In the name of God I depart, placing my trust in God. There is no power or strength except in God.

(M)

354

What should we say when we travel by car, bus or other means of transport: Glory be to the One Who has made it possible for us to master this (car, plane etc.) for our needs. Otherwise, we would not have been able to accomplish it on our own. And we will surely return to our Lord in the end.

The Quran

355

What should we say when we study: O Lord! Increase me in knowledge.

The Quran

356

What should we say when we face a problem: God is enough for us, and He is the best guardian and helper.

(B)

357

A supplication for all occasions: O Lord, I ask You to help me accomplish what is good and leave what is bad, and to have love for the poor and needy, and I ask You to forgive me and have mercy on me. I ask You for Your love, and for the love of those who love You, and for the love of deeds that will draw me closer to Your love.

(B)

358

My Lord, forgive me, and my parents and all the believers on the Day of Judgement.

The Quran

359

My Lord, have mercy on my parents, as they did care for me when I was little.

The Quran

360

O my Lord! I seek from You the strength and ability to do good, to shun sin and to help the poor. May You grant me deliverance and have mercy on me. Make me die before You put me to a test. I seek from You the strength and ability to love You and him who loves You and to prefer such acts which may draw me close to You.

Mustadrak

O my Lord! I am weak and helpless. Grant me the strength to do all that pleases You. Prompt me to do good enthusiastically. Make faith my goal. I am humble and disgraced; grant me honour and glory. I am resourceless; bless me with sustenance.

Mustadrak

362

O my Lord! I seek from You the ability to ask of You what is best for me: the best supplication, comprehensive success, abiding reward, and an enviable life record and death. Keep me steady. Enhance the scale of my good deeds. Strengthen my faith. Raise my rank. Accept my prayers. I ask of You the highest rank in Paradise.

Mustadrak

363

O God! Make my inner being better than my outer one and make me pious outwardly as well. I seek from You such good things as You grant—wealth, wives and children. Protect me from going astray. Let me not mislead anyone.

(T)

364

O God! Purify my heart of hypocrisy, my actions of pretence, my tongue of lies, and my eyes of deception. For You know well the deception of the eye and all that is concealed in the heart.

Kanz al-Ummal

365

O God! I seek from You wholesome sustenance, beneficial knowledge and such deeds as You accept.

al-Tabarani

JAICO PUBLISHING HOUSE

Elevate Your Life. Transform Your World.

ESTABLISHED IN 1946, Jaico Publishing House is home to world-transforming authors such as Sri Sri Paramahansa Yogananda, Osho, The Dalai Lama, Sri Sri Ravi Shankar, Robin Sharma, Deepak Chopra, Jack Canfield, Eknath Easwaran, Devdutt Pattanaik, Khushwant Singh, John Maxwell, Brian Tracy and Stephen Hawking.

Our late founder Mr. Jaman Shah first established Jaico as a book distribution company. Sensing that independence was around the corner, he aptly named his company Jaico ('Jai' means victory in Hindi). In order to service the significant demand for affordable books in a developing nation, Mr. Shah initiated Jaico's own publications. Jaico was India's first publisher of paperback books in the English language.

While self-help, religion and philosophy, mind/body/spirit, and business titles form the cornerstone of our non-fiction list, we publish an exciting range of travel, current affairs, biography, and popular science books as well. Our renewed focus on popular fiction is evident in our new titles by a host of fresh young talent from India and abroad. Jaico's recently established Translations Division translates selected English content into nine regional languages.

Jaico's Higher Education Division (HED) is recognized for its student-friendly textbooks in Business Management and Engineering which are in use countrywide.

In addition to being a publisher and distributor of its own titles, Jaico is a major national distributor of books of leading international and Indian publishers. With its headquarters in Mumbai, Jaico has branches and sales offices in Ahmedabad, Bangalore, Bhopal, Bhubaneswar, Chennai, Delhi, Hyderabad, Kolkata and Lucknow.

SINCE 1946

www.ingramcontent.com/pod-product-compliance
Ingram Content Group UK Ltd.
Pitfield, Milton Keynes, MK11 3LW, UK
UKHW021643190726
13853UKWH00001B/12